MICHIGAN

in words and pictures

BY DENNIS B. FRADIN

ILLUSTRATIONS BY RICHARD WAHL

MAPS BY LEN W. MEENTS

Consultant:
Richard M. Doolen
Assistant Director
Bently Historical Library
The University of Michigan, Ann Arbor

 CHILDRENS PRESS, CHICAGO

For my friends Karin and Tom Summers of Bessemer, Michigan

Lake Huron shoreline

Library of Congress Cataloging in Publication Data

Fradin, Dennis B.
  Michigan in words and pictures.

  SUMMARY: A brief history of the Wolverine State
with a description of its countryside and major cities.
  1. Michigan—Juvenile literature.   [1. Michigan]
I. Wahl, Richard, 1939-   II.   Meents, Len. W.
III. Title.
F566.3.F7   977.4   79-22356
ISBN 0-516-03922-9

1 2 3 4 5 6 7 8 9 10 11 12 R 87 86 85 84 83 82 81 80

PICTURE ACKNOWLEDGMENTS:
TRAVEL BUREAU, MICHIGAN DEPARTMENT OF COMMERCE—2, 10,
18, 19, 20, 23, 24 (left), 26, 27 (left), 28, 31 (left), 32, 33 (right), 34, 36
(right), 38, 39, 43
MICHIGAN TOURIST COUNCIL—Cover, 24 (right), 25, 33 (left), 35, 36
(left)
DEPARTMENT OF NATURAL RESOURCES—41 (left)
NATIONAL PARK SERVICE—37 (right: Richard Frear), 40 (M.
Woodbridge Williams)
JAMES P. ROWAN—29
NATIONAL MUSIC CAMP OF INTERLOCHEN CENTER FOR THE
ARTS—37 (left)
NEWS DEPARTMENT FORD MOTOR COMPANY—30
MICHIGAN BELL TELEPHONE CO.—22 (Robert Thom)
FMC CORPORATION—27 (right)
UNIVERSITY OF MICHIGAN INFORMATION SERVICES—31 (right)
UNIVERSITY NEWS BUREAU, NORTHERN MICHIGAN UNIVERSITY,
MARQUETTE—41 (right)
COVER—Lake Michigan

Michigan (MISH • ih • ghin) comes from the Chippewa (CHIP • ih • wa) word *Michigama* (mich • ih • GAHM • ah). It means *great lake.* Michigan borders on four of the five Great Lakes—Michigan, Huron (HYOOR • on), Erie (EE • ree), and Superior (soo • PEER • ee • ore).

Water divides Michigan into two parts. The northern part is known as the Upper Peninsula (pen • IN • soo • lah). The southern part is known as the Lower Peninsula. A peninsula is land that is almost surrounded by water.

Beautiful waters are just a part of Michigan. Michigan has farming. It has big cities like Detroit (dee • TROYT), where many things are made. Michigan also has copper and iron mining.

Do you know which state builds the most cars? Do you know where the most cherries are grown? Do you know where former President Gerald Ford grew up? As you will see, the answer to all these questions is Michigan.

Ages ago, all of Michigan was covered by water. The seas dried, leaving a lot of salt behind.

About a million years ago, the weather turned colder. The Ice Age began. Huge mountains of ice, called *glaciers* (GLAY • sherz), came down from the north. Most of Michigan was covered. The glaciers came to Michigan at least four times. The ice was up to two miles thick over the land. The glaciers ground off the tops of hills and crunched them into good rich soil. The glaciers also scooped out holes which filled with water and became lakes. The Great Lakes were made in this way. The Ice Age lasted until about 10,000 years ago.

Before there were people in Michigan, there were
some interesting animals. There were giant beavers.
They were as big as a grown man. There were
mammoths (MAM • uths) and mastodons (MAS • tuh • dons),
too. These hairy, tusked animals were related to
elephants.

Giant beavers, mammoths, and mastodons all died out
long ago.

The first people came to Michigan at least 8000 years ago. Bones of ancient people have been found in mounds built over 2000 years ago. Their stone spears and tools have been found, too.

In Michigan's Upper Peninsula ancient people learned how to mine copper. They made only a few copper tools. They may have used the copper as money. Why they went to so much trouble to mine the copper is still a mystery.

In the lower part of Michigan—known as the Lower Peninsula—"garden beds" have been found. These garden beds were built many hundreds of years ago. There are no signs that gardening was ever done on them. What were the garden beds used for? That is also a mystery.

Michigan scientists are still digging to learn more about the region's early people. These early people are thought to be related to the Indians who came later.

In more recent times, a number of Indian tribes lived (and some still live) in Michigan.

The Chippewa, Wyandot (WHY • an • dot), and Menominee (mi • NOM • in • ee) Indians lived mainly in the Upper Peninsula. The Ottawa (OT • a • wah), Potawatomi (pot • ah • WOT • ah • mee), and Miami (my • AM • ee) lived mainly in the Lower Peninsula. The Indians of Michigan lived peacefully.

Most Indian villages were near rivers or lakes. Most Indians lived in wigwams—round houses made of poles and tree bark. The Indians fished with bone hooks. The Chippewa built fine birch canoes.

The Indians gathered blueberries, blackberries, and acorns in the woods. In the Upper Peninsula the Chippewa and Menominee gathered wild rice.

Indian women grew corn and beans. The men hunted with bows and arrows or spears. They hunted bears, deer, and beaver. Animals provided more than meat. Moccasins, clothes, and blankets were made out of the animal skins.

Michigan Indians gathered shells, which they made into beads called *wampum*. They used strings of wampum for belts, ornaments, and money. Indians didn't write yet. So they sent messages with wampum pictures. If one tribe wanted to show friendship for another, they might send a belt showing two people holding hands.

The Indians believed in many nature gods. There were gods of the sky, woods, and lakes.

The French were the first explorers in Michigan. France ruled Canada. Etienne Brulé (ay • TYEN broo • LAY) is thought to be the first explorer in Michigan. About 1620, Brulé paddled into Lake Superior. He explored the shores of the eastern Upper Peninsula. In 1634 the French explorer Jean Nicolet (ZHAN nee • ko • LAY) came. He explored other parts of the Upper Peninsula, after he sailed through the Straits of Mackinac (MAK • in • naw). In 1669 Adrien Jolliet (AY •

dree • en zhol • ee • AY) explored the eastern shore of the Lower Peninsula. In 1671 France claimed Michigan.

French priests came. They built churches, called *missions*. In 1641 the priests Raymbault (raym • BOH) and Jogues (ZHOHG) visited the Chippewa. The priests named the place they visited Sault Sainte Marie (SOO SAYNT mah • REE). The first settlement in Michigan was built in 1668 by Father Jacques Marquette (ZHAHK mar • KETT), at Sault Sainte Marie.

Sault Sainte Marie

French fur traders came. They traded pots, pans, and trinkets to the Indians. In return the traders received beaver and other furs. Most Indians were friendly to the Frenchmen.

In 1701 the French soldier Antoine Cadillac (AN • twon CAD • i • lak) built a fort in southeast Michigan. It grew into a town—Detroit.

England—which ruled the colonies in the East—also wanted to trade with the Indians. England and France went to war over a huge piece of land that included Michigan. In 1763 England won this war (called the French and Indian War.) England now ruled Michigan.

The Indians and the French had often liked each other. But the Indians disliked the English. The English treated them badly. Pontiac (PON • tee • ack), chief of the Ottawa, formed a large army. The Indians fought the English and took over their forts. To take Fort Michilimackinac (mish • ill • ih • MACK • in • naw), the Indians tricked the

English. The Indians played a ball game called lacrosse
outside the fort. The soldiers left the fort to watch the
game. Meanwhile, Indian women slipped inside the fort.
They had hidden knives and tomahawks under their
blankets. The Indian men threw their ball near the gate.
They pretended to chase the ball, but ran inside the fort
instead. They grabbed the weapons and killed the
English soldiers.

The Indians under Pontiac captured every English fort
except Detroit. The Indians fought at Detroit for almost
six months, but they could not take it. Finally, Pontiac
had to give up. He signed a peace treaty with the
English.

England did not have Michigan for long. In 1776 a new country had been formed—the United States of America. To become free of England, the United States fought and won the Revolutionary War (rev • oh • LOO • shun • airy wore). In 1783 Michigan became part of the United States. Michigan wasn't a state yet. In 1787 it was part of the Northwest Territory. In 1805 Michigan became a separate territory.

NORTHWEST TERRITORY

But the United States wasn't finished fighting with England. During the War of 1812, United States and England fought again. In one battle, Oliver Hazard Perry defeated the English on Lake Erie. After the War of 1812, the United States was in control of Michigan.

Few Americans came to Michigan at first. "It's good-for-nothing swamp land," people said. Lewis Cass helped prove them wrong. He was governor of the Michigan Territory from 1813-31. In 1820 he explored Michigan by canoe and horseback. He made treaties with the Indians, getting them to turn over their land. Cass learned that Michigan had fine forests and rich farmland.

The word went out: "There's good farmland in Michigan." But it was hard to get to Michigan. In 1825 the Erie Canal opened. It was in far-away New York. But it was important to Michigan. It meant that people could go to Michigan by boat.

Thanks to the Erie Canal, many farmers came to Michigan. They grew wheat and corn. They learned how to grow apples, peaches, and cherries. In places where many farmers settled, small towns grew.

Lumberjacks arrived, too. They cut the trees into logs. The logs were taken by sleds to rivers such as the Muskegon (mus • KEE • gun) and Saginaw. The logs sat by the frozen waters all winter. When the ice in the rivers melted, the lumberjacks drove the logs to the sawmills. Michigan wood was called "Green Gold" because it was so good for building.

In the early 1830s, many people wanted Michigan to become a state. But there was a problem. Michigan and Ohio lawmakers were arguing over a piece of land, called the Toledo Strip. The United States Congress decided this argument. Ohio got the land. Michigan was given the Upper Peninsula, which had been part of the Wisconsin Territory. "The U.P. is worthless," said many Michigan people. Later they learned that they were very wrong.

On January 26, 1837, Michigan became our 26th state. Detroit was the capital for the state's first ten years. (Lansing became the capital in 1847.) The state's first governor was Stevens T. Mason. He was called the "Boy Governor" because when he was only 19 years old he was acting governor of the territory. Michigan became known as the *Wolverine State* because of the wolverine furs that were once traded there.

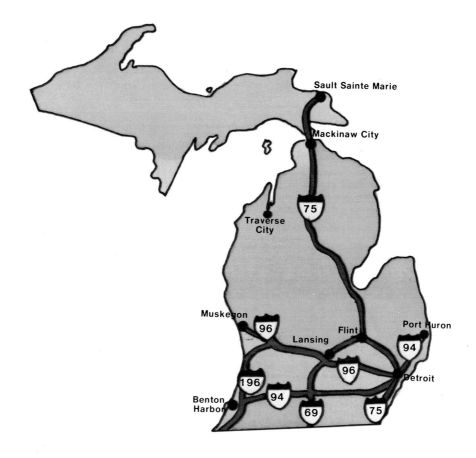

Michigan people found out how wrong they were about the Upper Peninsula. In the 1830s Dr. Douglass Houghton (HOO • tin) found copper there. Copper is valuable. It is used to make coins, machines, and wire. Copper mines were opened. Soon the northern part of the U.P. became known as the "Treasure Chest."

Iron was found near Negaunee (neh • GAWN • ee) and Ishpeming (ISH • pih • ming) in 1844. Steel mills were hungry for this iron. The problem was that boats could not carry the iron directly to the steel mills. There was no water passage between Lake Superior and Lake Huron. Lake Superior is higher. The water from Lake Superior flows into Lake Huron in a series of rapids on the St. Marys River. Big boats could not shoot down those rapids. To solve this problem, the Soo Ship Canal was built in 1855. At the canal, ships are raised and lowered so they can pass from Lake Superior to Lake Huron. Ships filled with Michigan iron could now go to the great steel cities.

Soo Locks

Ships pass through the Soo Locks

An important event happened in Michigan in 1854. On July 6 a group of people who disliked slavery held a meeting at Jackson. They started a new political party in the United States. They called it the Republican Party.

Slavery was one of the issues when the Northern states fought the Southern states during the Civil War (1861-1865). About 92,000 Michigan men fought for the North. Soldiers from Michigan captured Jefferson Davis, president of the Southern states.

Kellogg's headquarters at Battle Creek

Michigan had been a lumbering, farming, and mining state. After the Civil War, Michigan began to become a manufacturing state, too. Many things were made in Michigan.

Two men, C.W. Post and W.K. Kellogg turned the making of breakfast cereal into big business. Battle Creek became known as the *Cereal Center of the World*.

In the 1870s Grand Rapids became a big furniture-making city. Chairs, tables, and beds were made there. Grand Rapids became known as the *Furniture Capital of America*.

There was a bad part to all this manufacturing in Michigan. By 1900, many forests were gone. Other Michigan forests were destroyed by fire. In 1881 a huge forest fire destroyed many towns and killed 125 people in southeast Michigan.

In the 1900s new trees were planted in Michigan. Laws were passed to save the forests. Look-out stations were built so that rangers could watch for forest fires.

In the late 1890s and early 1900s Michigan men built some of the first automobiles. In 1896 Henry Ford drove his car around Detroit. Ransom Olds drove his car around Lansing in that same year. Some people laughed at these sputtering, slow-moving cars. "Get a horse!" they said. Better and faster cars were made. Ransom Olds began making Oldsmobiles in Detroit. People bought the cars as fast as he could make them. At first only a few cars were built each year. Olds started making his cars on assembly lines. Many people—each with a job to do—worked on putting the cars together. It

"Putting the World on Wheels," painting of Detroit in 1913

took less time that way. In 1903 the Olds factory made 5000 cars. Henry Ford formed his Ford Motor Company in Detroit in 1903. In 1908 Ford began making the famous Model T car on assembly lines. David Buick and the Dodge brothers also began making cars in the Detroit area.

Detroit became known as the *Motor City*. It grew into Michigan's biggest city. Cities near Detroit—such as Flint and Dearborn—also became auto-making cities.

Mackinac Bridge

During World War I (1914-1918) the army needed tanks, airplane motors, and trucks. Detroit had the workers and the assembly lines. So Detroit did the job. During World War II (1939-1945) Detroit made jeeps, tanks, and airplanes.

In 1957 a five-mile-long bridge linking the Upper Peninsula to the Lower Peninsula was completed. It is called the Mackinac Bridge. But it is nicknamed "Big Mac."

Today, Michigan is still an important farming, mining, and manufacturing state.

You have learned about some of Michigan's interesting history. Now it is time for a trip—in words and pictures—through the *Wolverine State*.

One of Michigan's nicknames is *Water Wonderland*. The glaciers left the state 11,000 lakes. Michigan's waters and rivers make it a leading vacation state.

Lumberjacks used to tell stories about how Michigan's lakes got there. They said a giant lumberjack, named Paul Bunyan, dug the lakes himself so he would have a place to store the millions of logs he cut down.

Right: Fisherman shows off his Chinook salmon
Below: Lake Superior sunset

Fall in Keweenaw County

Today, over half of Michigan is still wooded. The farther north you go the more forests you'll see. Hiking through the woods or driving on a woodland road you may see deer peeking out at you. Bears, bobcats, and foxes also live in the forests. But there are only a few wolves left in Michigan.

The southern part of Michigan is often called the Lower Peninsula. The state's biggest cities—Detroit, Grand Rapids, Flint, Warren, and Lansing—are here.

Detroit is in southeastern Michigan. It lies along the Detroit River. Canada is across the Detroit River.

Detroit was founded by the French soldier Antoine Cadillac in 1701. He built a fort. French fur traders came there to trade with the Indians. A little settlement grew there.

What would Antoine Cadillac think if he saw Detroit today? It is the biggest city in Michigan—by far. And it is one of the biggest cities in the entire United States.

There are over 100 million cars on U.S. streets. Many of them were made in Detroit, which is often called the

Detroit skyline

Above: Auto plant, Dearborn
Right: Chemical packaging plant in Livonia

Motor City. Cars are also assembled in other Michigan cities, some of them very close to Detroit. You can visit auto plants to see how cars are made. Thousands of people work in these auto factories.

Paint, chemicals, and hardware are also made in Detroit. Many of these products go by boat, truck, or train to other cities in America.

Detroit has some interesting museums. At the Detroit Historical Museum you can see how the city looked over 100 years ago. At the Afro-American Museum you can learn about famous black people and African history. At the Detroit Institute of Arts you can see some of the world's great paintings.

Renaissance
Center

Detroit has some fine new buildings—such as the Civic
Center and Cobo Hall. But many of Detroit's people have
been living in old, run-down buildings. In recent years
some of those old buildings have been torn down. New
ones have gone up.

Detroit is a big sports town. In the summer, you can
see the Detroit Tigers play baseball. In the fall, the
Detroit Lions play football. In the winter you can see the
Detroit Red Wings play hockey or the Detroit Pistons
play basketball.

Detroit also has some famous zoos. At Belle Isle there
is a zoo especially for children. You can pet the animals
there. The Detroit Zoo is one of the world's best.

Dearborn is just west of Detroit. The Ford Motor Company has its main factory there. Visit the Henry Ford Museum in Dearborn. There you can learn about the history of the car, airplane, and other inventions. At the museum called Greenfield Village you can see the homes of the Wright brothers, Thomas Edison, and other inventors. Henry Ford moved these homes here. He wanted people to remember America's great inventors. There are many other buildings at Greenfield Village that show how America looked in the past. You can tour Greenfield Village in an old Model T car.

Above: Carriage at Greenfield Village
Left: 1876 Mason Engine at Greenfield Village

Assembly line at a Ford plant

The city of Warren is just outside Detroit, too.
Settlers and fur trappers once had to kill bears and
wolves to keep the town safe. Glass, steel, and plastics
for cars are made in Warren today.

Pontiac is about 25 miles northwest of Detroit. It was
named after Chief Pontiac. Cars are put together in
Pontiac.

Flint is about 60 miles northwest of Detroit. Flint
started out as a fur-trading center. Then it became a
lumber town. Today, Flint, too, is part of the auto-
making business.

Above: Angell Hall, University of Michigan,
Ann Arbor
Left: Flint

Ann Arbor is about 38 miles west of Detroit. Two
women who lived here in the town's early days were
named Ann. Ann Arbor was named after them. The
University of Michigan is at Ann Arbor. Students at the
University of Michigan study many subjects. The school
is also famous for its football team.

Lansing is the capital of Michigan. In the 1840s
Michigan people decided that the capital should be
nearer to the center of the state than Detroit. Where
should the capital be? The people argued and argued.

State Capitol, Lansing

Finally, in 1847 they picked Lansing. Only one log house and one sawmill were in Lansing at the time. Many thought the idea was a joke. But the forest was cleared and Lansing became the capital. State lawmakers went to meet there.

Cars are still made in this city where Ransom Olds drove one of the first "horseless carriages."

Michigan State University is in East Lansing. There, students learn about farming and many other subjects.

Above: Calder sculpture, Grand Rapids
Left: Grand Rapids

Grand Rapids is about 62 miles west of Lansing. Grand Rapids is Michigan's second biggest city. Like many other Michigan cities, Grand Rapids started out as a fur-trading post. French people traded with Ottawa Indians in the area. The first settler was a woman. Her name was Madame LaFramboise (la Fram • BWAHZ), and she traded with the Indians here for about 50 years. The town was founded in 1827 by Louis Campau (Loo • ee Kam • POH), a fur trader.

Later, logging became important in the Grand Rapids area. Lumberjacks drove logs down the Grand River to Grand Rapids mills. Pine, oak, and maple came to the mills. There, they were made into furniture.

Grand Rapids is still known as the *"Furniture Capital of America."* The chair you sit in and the bed you sleep in may have been made in Grand Rapids.

Gerald Ford grew up in Grand Rapids. He became president of the United States in 1974.

The Lower Peninsula has most of the state's farms. Michigan farmers raise beef cattle. Others raise dairy cattle. Corn, peaches, apples, strawberries, navy beans, plums, soybeans, and wheat are some of Michigan's crops. The area along Lake Michigan is good for growing

Dairy farm

Above: Peaches
Right: Apples

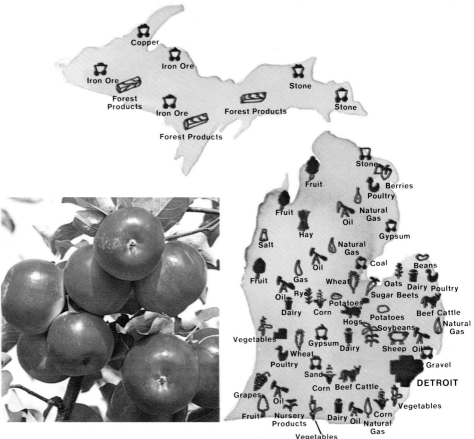

fruit. Think of Michigan the next time you eat a cherry

pie. Michigan farmers grow the most cherries of any

state. Many foods grown in western Michigan are sent to

Grand Rapids. From Grand Rapids these foods go out by

train and truck to feed people across America.

A trip up the eastern shore of Lake Michigan will

take you to many interesting places.

Holland is a town that was founded by Dutch people.

They wanted to make their town look like their old

homes across the ocean. They brought a windmill from

Tulip Festival dancers

Windmill Island, Holland

Holland. There is even a factory in the town that makes wooden shoes. Every May, the people of Holland, Michigan hold a Tulip Festival. There are parades. And people dance in wooden shoes.

Farther north, visit the National Music Camp at Interlochen (IN • ter • lock • in). Every summer, young people come here to study music.

There are many sand dunes (hills) along Lake Michigan. The Sleeping Bear Dune at Glen Haven is the biggest sand dune in the world.

Above: Sleeping Bear Dune
Left: Interlochen National Music Camp
orchestra

The Chippewa and Ottawa Indians told a story about this dune. According to the story, a big forest fire in Wisconsin forced a black bear and her two cubs to swim across Lake Michigan. When they neared shore, the cubs got tired and drowned. The tired mother bear climbed to the beach to wait for her cubs. The gods felt sorry for the sad mother bear. They raised the drowned cubs from the water and turned them into islands. The gods covered the mother bear with sand and she became the Sleeping Bear Dune.

Above: Grand Hotel, Mackinac Island
Right: Main Street, Mackinac Island

On your way to the Upper Peninsula, go to Mackinac Island. It is in the Straits of Mackinac. You can get there by boat. Everything is green and lovely on Mackinac Island. You can't travel about the island by car. Cars aren't allowed there. But you can take a horse and buggy ride. Visit Fort Mackinac, built by the English in 1780. The Indians told many stories about this lovely island. According to the Ottawa, one their great spirits lived in the sky. This god was named Nanabozho (non • ah • BOZ • ho) and he created people and earth. Sometimes he liked to come down to earth for a visit. While on earth he stayed on Mackinac Island.

Northern Michigan is called the Upper Peninsula. It does not have much farmland. It does not have any big cities. The biggest, Marquette, has only about 24,000 people.

The north *does* have a lot of mining. Iron and copper are mined. Night and day, the miners take these metals from the earth.

The region also has vast forests. Most of the lumbering done in Michigan today is in the Upper Peninsula.

The Upper Peninsula has waterfalls, such as Agate and Tahquamenon (tah • KWAH • meh • non) Falls. It has

Tahquamenon Falls

Miners Castle, Pictured Rocks

beautiful mountains. People like to ski at Iron Mountain, Indianhead, and Big Powderhorn. At Copper Peak, experts "ski fly" through the air.

Much of the Upper Peninsula is still wilderness. You are likely to see deer crossing the road. The air in the north country is fresh and sweet with the smell of pine — except when there's a skunk in the road!

Take a boat ride along the shore of Lake Superior. Near Munising you can see the tall cliffs, called Pictured Rocks. The rocks have many different colors. Glaciers, waves, and wind have carved them into strange shapes

Above: Deer
Left: Bobcat

over millions of years. The Chippewa Indians said that the lightning and thunder gods lived inside the caves in the rocks. You can see Rainbow Cave, Miner's Castle, Flower Vase Rock, and Chapel Rock.

The Porcupine Mountains are in Porcupine Mountains Wilderness State Park. Porcupines, bears, and deer live in the "Porkies." From high up on a cliff you can see one of the most beautiful sights in Michigan—Lake of the Clouds. The still waters of the lake reflect the sky like a mirror.

The Porkies are very near the southern shore of Lake Superior. Lake Superior is a clear, clean lake. Even in the summer it is very cold.

Michigan has a number of islands in Lake Michigan and Lake Superior. Isle Royale in Lake Superior is Michigan's biggest island. It is about 50 miles from Houghton. Cars are not allowed on Isle Royale. You can see where Indians once mined copper. There is a large herd of moose on Isle Royale. There are some timber wolves, too. In 1912 Lake Superior froze over. The moose and wolves are thought to have crossed over the ice from Canada. Hunting is not allowed on the island, so it is a perfect home for these animals.

Lake of the Clouds, Porcupine Mountains

Land of waterfalls ... beautiful lakes ... and forests ...

Home to Indians ... fur trappers ... farmers ... and lumberjacks ...

Land of the *Motor City* ... the *Furniture Capital of America* ... the *Cereal Center of the World* ...

Home to Henry Ford ... Gerald Ford ... and the "Boy Governor" ...

This is Michigan—the *Wolverine State.*

Facts About MICHIGAN

Area—58,216 square miles (23rd biggest state)

Greatest Distance North to South—285 miles in Lower Peninsula
215 miles in Upper Peninsula

Greatest Distance East to West—200 miles in Lower Peninsula
334 miles in Upper Peninsula

Highest Point—1,980 feet above sea level (Mt. Curwood)

Lowest Point—572 feet above sea level (along shore of Lake Erie)

Hottest Recorded Temperature—112° F. (at Mio on July 13, 1936)

Coldest Recorded Temperature—Minus 51° F. (at Vanderbilt, on
February 9, 1934)

Statehood—Our 26th state, on January 26, 1937

Origin of Name Michigan—From the Chippewa Indian word *Michigama,*
meaning "great lake"

Capital—Lansing (1847)

Previous Capital—Detroit

Counties—83

U.S. Senators—2

U.S. Representatives—19

Electoral Votes—21

State Senators—38

State Representatives—110

State Song—"Michigan, My Michigan"

State Motto—*Si quaeris peninsulam amoenam, circumspice* (Latin
meaning "If you seek a pleasant peninsula, look about you.")

Nicknames—Wolverine State, Water Wonderland

State Seal—Adopted in 1835

State Flag—Adopted in 1911

State Flower—Apple blossom

State Bird—Robin

State Tree—White pine

State Fish—Brook trout

State Stone—Petoskey Stone

State Gem—Isle Royale Greenstone (Chlorastrolite)

Some Rivers—St. Marys, Escanaba, Manistique, Menominee, Sturgeon,
Tahquamenon, Whitefish, Ontonagan, Grand, Muskegon, Saginaw, Detroit,
St. Clair, Cass

Some Waterfalls—Agate, Laughing Whitefish, Miners, Munising, Upper and
Lower Tahquamenon Falls

Largest Lake Inside State—Houghton Lake

Largest Island—Isle Royale

Animals—Deer, black bears, badgers, bobcats, minks, muskrats, porcupine,
wolves, red foxes, otters, opossums, ducks, pheasants, grouse, geese,
partridges

Fishing—Trout, pike, perch, bass, crappie, smelt, catfish, whitefish

Isle Royale
National Park

Porcupine Mtn.

Pictured Rocks
National Lakeshore

Hiawatha National Fore
Sault Sainte Mar

Ottawa
National Forest

Hiawatha
National
Forest

Mackinaw City

National
Lakeshore

Huron Nation
Fore

Manistee
National
Forest

Lansing

Kalamazoo River

Detro

44

Farm Products—Cherries, apples, corn, soybeans, navy beans, wheat, sugar
    beets, grapes, peaches, plums, pears, strawberries, potatoes, tomatoes,
    sweet corn, alfalfa, celery, milk, eggs, beef cattle, turkeys, hogs

Mining—Iron, copper, salt, oil, natural gas

Manufacturing Products—Cars, trucks, buses, breakfast cereal, baby foods,
    many other food products, chemicals, furniture, clothes, sporting goods,
    glass products, rubber products, plastic products

Population—9,129,000 (1977 estimate)

Major Cities—

Detroit	1,210,000	(all 1979 estimates)
Grand Rapids	180,500	
Warren	166,300	
Flint	160,600	
Lansing	123,000	
Livonia	110,800	
Ann Arbor	106,200	

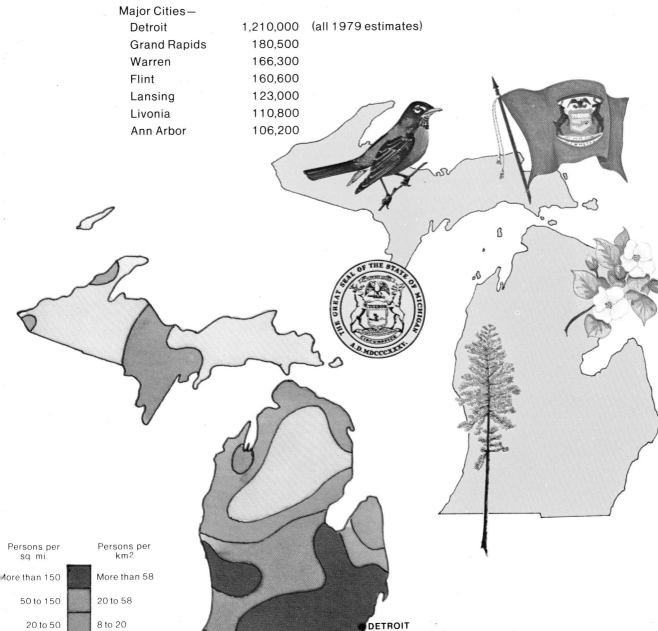

Persons per sq. mi.	Persons per km²
More than 150	More than 58
50 to 150	20 to 58
20 to 50	8 to 20
Less than 20	Less than 8

DETROIT

The History of Michigan

There were people in Michigan at least 8000 years ago.

1620—About this time French explorer Etienne Brulé comes to Michigan

1634—Jean Nicolet sails through Straits of Mackinac

1641—Raymbault and Jogues visit Sault Ste. Marie

1668—First settlement in Michigan built by Father Jacques Marquette at Sault Ste. Marie

1669—Adrien Jolliet explores Lower Peninsula

1671—St. Lusson claims region for King of France

1701—Antoine Cadillac founds Detroit

1763—England controls Michigan after French and Indian War

1763—Indians under Chief Pontiac take many forts

1765—Pontiac signs peace treaty with English at Detroit

1783—Michigan is part of new country—United States of America!

1787—Michigan is part of Northwest Territory of the United States

1805—The Territory of Michigan is created by U.S. Congress

1812—War of 1812 begins: England against United States

1813—Oliver Hazard Perry beats English on Lake Erie

1814—War of 1812 ends

1819—Governor Lewis Cass obtains Indian lands for Michigan in Treaty of Saginaw

1821—Cass obtains more Indian lands

1825—Erie Canal opens, making it easier to get to Michigan from the East

1837—Michigan becomes our 26th state on January 26th; Michigan gets Upper Peninsula after losing other land to Ohio; Stevens T. Mason is Michigan's first governor; Detroit is first capital

1840—Dr. Douglass Houghton finds copper in Upper Peninsula

1841—University of Michigan opens at Ann Arbor

1844—Iron is found in Upper Peninsula

1847—Lansing is named capital

1848—Michigan lawmakers meet for first time in new capital, Lansing

1850—Population of Michigan is 397,654

1854—The Republican Party is formed at Jackson

1855—Soo Ship Canal and Locks are completed at Sault Ste. Marie

1870—Michigan becomes leading lumber state and keeps title for 20 years

1871—Huge forest fires in Michigan

1881—More forest fires

1890—Population is 2,093,889

1896—Henry Ford drives his car around Detroit and Ransom Olds drives his in Lansing

1899—Ransom Olds builds auto factory in Detroit, develops first assembly line for making cars

1900—Population of Michigan is 2,420,982

1908—Henry Ford begins making Model T cars

1914—Ford Motor Company decides to pay workers at least $5 for a day's work; this is high pay at the time

1914-1918—World War I; 135,485 Michigan men fight

1935—United Automobile Workers Union is formed

1937—Happy 100th birthday, Wolverine State!

1939-1945—Word War II; about 673,000 Michigan men and women in uniform

1945—Detroit Tigers win World Series, just as they did in 1935 and will do again in 1968

1957—Mackinac Bridge opens, linking Upper and Lower Peninsulas

1967—Forty-three people die in race riot in Detroit

1968—Michigan lawmakers battle water pollution

1969—William G. Milliken becomes governor

1970—Population of Michigan is 8,875,083

1976—Pontiac Stadium is completed

1978—Milliken is elected governor again

INDEX

About the Author:

Dennis Fradin attended Northwestern University on a creative writing scholarship and graduated in 1967. While still at Northwestern, he published his first stories in *Ingenue* magazine and also won a prize in *Seventeen's* short story competition. A prolific writer, Dennis Fradin has been regularly publishing stories in such diverse places as *The Saturday Evening Post, Scholastic, National Humane Review, Midwest,* and *The Teaching Paper.* He has also scripted several educational films. Since 1970 he has taught second grade reading in a Chicago school—a rewarding job, which, the author says, "provides a captive audience on whom I test my children's stories." Married and the father of three children, Dennis Fradin spends his free time with his family or playing a myriad of sports and games with his childhood chums.

About the Artists:

Len Meents studied painting and drawing at Southern Illinois University and after graduation in 1969 he moved to Chicago. Mr. Meents works full time as a painter and illustrator. He and his wife and child currently make their home in LaGrange, Illinois.

Richard Wahl, graduate of the Art Center College of Design in Los Angeles, has illustrated a number of magazine articles and booklets. He is a skilled artist and photographer who advocates realistic interpretations of his subjects. He lives with his wife and two sons in Libertyville, Illinois.